I0161101

THE ALABAMA HISTORICAL SOCIETY
MONTGOMERY
Reprint No. 26

Revolutionary Soldiers

Buried in Alabama

BY

MRS. PATRICK HUES MELL

[From the TRANSACTIONS 1899-1903, Vol. IV]

MONTGOMERY, ALABAMA

1904

Notice

In many older books, foxing (or discoloration) occurs and, in some instances, print lightens with wear and age. Reprinted books, such as this, often duplicate these flaws, notwithstanding efforts to reduce or eliminate them. The pages of this reprint have been digitally enhanced and, where possible, the flaws eliminated in order to provide clarity of content and a pleasant reading experience.

Revolutionary Soldiers Buried in Alabama

Excerpted from the *TRANSACTIONS 1899-1903, Volume IV*; by Mrs. Patrick Hues Mell, Published by The Alabama Historical Society, 1904

Originally published
Montgomery, Alabama
1904

Reprinted by:

Janaway Publishing, Inc.
2412 Nicklaus Dr.
Santa Maria, California 93455
(805) 925-1038
www.janawaygenealogy.com

2009

ISBN 10: 1-59641-187-2
ISBN 13: 978-1-59641-187-6

Made in the United States of America

Publisher's Preface

This booklet has been excerpted from The Alabama
Historical Society's *TRANSACTIONS 1899-
1903, Volume IV*; by Mrs. Patrick Hues Mell,
Published 1904, and includes pages 527 to 572 of the
original volume. This work retains those original
page numbers.

Janaway Publishing, Inc.

X. REVOLUTIONARY SOLDIERS BURIED IN ALABAMA.

"Names that adorn and dignify the scroll,
Whose leaves contain the nation's history."
—*Fitz Greene Halleck.*

By Mrs. P. H. Mell, Clemson College, S. C.
Late State Historian, Alabama Division, Daughters of the American Revolution.

The writer offers these brief biographical sketches of Revolutionary soldiers, pioneer settlers of Alabama, with the hope that they may prove of interest to the citizens now living in the State. These soldiers came to Alabama when this country, now so rich and populous, was a wilderness of dense forests and swamps, peopled by savages and wild animals. Trees fell before the sturdy strokes of their axes, lands were cleared 'and cabins built; so homes were made and bravely defended, and law and order began to reign over the land.

In studying the early history of any country it is of importance to know the characteristics of the settlers; not only the popular leaders, but representatives of all walks of life, for the sum total of individual histories and individual opinions makes up the history and politics of the State. When the majority of the first settlers are law-abiding, patriotic men of good sense and firm principles, then the State will find her growth and prosperity assured.

For a period of years after the Revolution, Alabama was anything but "a land of rest." The French struggle was over, but Spaniards, English, Americans and Indians contended for the mastery of the territory. This is probably the reason why there are no Revolutionary land grants to be found in the State. During the Revolution the white inhabitants of Alabama were loyal to the crown and therefore they were not entitled to bounty lands. The thirteen original States gave liberally to their soldiers. Ohio, Kentucky and Tennessee were thickly peopled with old soldiers and their families who settled on bounty lands. But there were no free lands in Alabama, prices were high and in 1819 public lands

(527)

sold for as much or more at the sales in Huntsville and St. Stephens as the same land would bring to-day.

We therefore know that only a few hundred Revolutionary soldiers settled in Alabama, while there were thousands in Ohio, Kentucky and Tennessee. In 1840, Alabama has a list of only one hundred and eighty-nine in the United States *Census of Pensioners,* while Kentucky has over nine hundred and other States correspondingly large numbers.

The Alabama Daughters of the American Revolution are endeavoring to locate and mark as many of the graves of these soldiers as possible and also to learn something of the history of each soldier. This is a difficult task, for early histories of the first years of the State are condensed and bare of details, only prominent men and notable events being described. To find out anything about these heroes involves researches in family records, old newspapers, the few local histories which have been published, and inscriptions on tombstones in city cemeteries, country churchyards, and old plantation family burial grounds. This work will be continued from year to year until Alabama has been thoroughly explored for the last resting places of these pioneer heroes.

In preparing these sketches the writer is indebted for valuable information to Hon. Thomas M. Owen, Secretary of the Alabama Historical Society, and Director of the Department of Archives and History of Alabama; to the regents and members of the Alabama Daughters of the American Revolution chapters and also to the descendants of some of the soldiers.

CAPTAIN WILLIAM ARMISTEAD.

"Though mixed with earth their perishable clay,
　Their names shall live while glory lives to tell
True to their country how they won the day."

The grave of this soldier is described in Ball's *Clarke County, Alabama,* pp. 475-6. We learn that a Capt. William Armistead of Virginia and three sons, Robert, Westwood and John, became citizens of Clarke. The father was a man of strong peculiarities, a gentleman of the old school, wearing knee buckles and retaining English tastes. He was twice married and had three sons and three daughters. One daughter married John Morriss, in North Carolina, and moved to Alabama; another daughter married Edmund Waddell, in North Carolina; the third married Dr. Neal Smith, a gentleman of prominence in his day.

The grave stands alone, neatly enclosed with rocks and pickets on a hill near Amity church in the family burial ground, on the plantation bequeathed by him to his son-in-law, Dr. Neal Smith, about eight miles from Grove Hill.

The following is a copy from the marble slab:

In
memory of
CAPTAIN WILLIAM ARMISTEAD,
a soldier of the
Revolution, a native
of Virginia,
who departed this life
March 1st, 1842,
aged 80 years.

The following notes on the family and ancestry of Capt. William Armistead are taken from the *William and Mary Quarterly*,[1] vols. vi, vii, viii:

Capt. William Armistead was doubtless a son of Anthony Armistead and brother of Anthony, Robert, Westwood and Alexander Carver. Two of his brothers were killed in the Revolution.

---

[1] It is to be regretted that so exhaustive and learned a genealogy as President Tyler has prepared should be marred by so palpable an error as his suggestion that Captain William Armistead was the son of Anthony Armistead[8]; since he gives from the records the names of the latter's children by Mary, his wife, who long survived her husband (as the wife of one Williams), and William is not one of them; the supposition that he married, secondly, Elizabeth Lee, is out of the question.

Tyler's genealogy is so complete that he not only proves Capt. William Armistead *not* to have been a son of Anthony[8], but not even a grandson of Lieutenant-Colonel Anthony[4].

There is no doubt in my mind that our Revolutionary soldier was a grandson of Anthony Armistead, of Warwick, son of William, a brother of Lieutenant-Colonel Anthony[4]—for the locality of his birth, the names of his children (Westwood and Starkey), the ownership of land in North Carolina by that branch of the family and his own removal thither, are strong presumptive reasons for the belief; and they are clinched by the evident impossibility of his having been the grandson of Anthony[4], of Elizabeth City. Note, especially, that while the Westwoods were kinsmen of both the Elizabeth City and Warwick families, the Starkeys were kin to the latter alone.

It must be remembered that Elizabeth City and Warwick counties are adjacent, and together form but a small territory.

I hope to be able, in a short time, to contribute a note clarifying the question: who was Capt. Armistead's father?—W. B. NEWMAN, of Talladega, Ala.

He saw his brother Westwood killed at the battle of Brandywine; and he himself joined the army when only sixteen years of age. We will give his line of descent from this interesting Virginia family.

(1) ANTHONY ARMISTEAD, of Kirk Deighton, Yorkshire, and Frances Thompson, his wife, of the same place, had issue:

(2) WILLIAM ARMISTEAD, baptized Aug. 3, 1610, in "All Saints Church," the only church in the parish of Kirk Deighton. He emigrated to Virginia about 1635, and obtained large grants of land in Elizabeth City county, and subsequently, Gloucester county. He died before 1660. He married Anne ———— and had issue, among others:

(3) ANTHONY ARMISTEAD, ancestor of President Tyler, resided in Elizabeth City county. He was one of Sir William Berkeley's court-martial in 1676 to try the Bacon insurgents, justice of the peace, and captain of horse in 1680, burgess in 1693, 1696, 1699, and one of the committee in 1700 to report a revision of the laws, which was approved by the general assembly in 1705. Capt. Armistead married Hannah, daughter of Dr. Robert Ellyson, of James City county. This Robert Ellyson appears in the Maryland records as early as 1643 as "barber-chirurgeon" and after holding the office of sheriff of St. Mary's, emigrated to Virginia, where he was high sheriff of James City county, sergeant-at-arms of the house of burgesses in 1657-58, and a leading burgess in 1656, 1659-60, 1660-61, 1663, with the rank of captain. The wife of Capt. Anthony Armistead survived him, her will being proved in Elizabeth City court in 1728. They had issue, among others:

(4) ANTHONY ARMISTEAD, lieut.-col. of militia in 1724, justice and high sheriff of Elizabeth City county, married, it is believed twice; first, Anne, who united with Anthony Armistead in a deed in 1717; second, Elizabeth Westwood, sister of William Westwood. Anthony Armistead's will was proved Dec. 18, 1728. He had children; several daughters who were affectionately remembered by their nephew, Capt. William Armistead. One of his sons:

(5) ANTHONY ARMISTEAD married Mary, daughter of Anthony Tucker and Rosea, his wife. It is thought that there was a second marriage to Elizabeth Lee and that Capt. William Armistead was a child of this marriage. A family of Lees has long re-

sided in the neighborhood of Elizabeth City county. Issue, among others:

(6) WILLIAM ARMISTEAD, the subject of this sketch, born 1762, died 1842. We append a copy of his Revolutionary services taken from the archives at Washington and sent to us with other information by his descendant, Mrs. Sallie Jones Featherston, of Rome, Ga. After the Revolution he moved to Warren, thence to Randolph county, North Carolina, and married (1) Rebecca Kimbell, near Warrenton. The family Bible gives authentic information for the births of their children: 1. Westwood, born Aug. 24, 1791; 2. John Kimbell, born Dec. 16, 1792; 3. Elizabeth Lee, born Oct. 13, 1794; 4. Martha, born Sept. 1, 1796. He married (2) Elizabeth, widow of John Morriss and daughter of Mr. Lewis and his wife, Jane Westmoreland, of Halifax county, Va. His second wife had one son by her first husband, John Morriss. Issue by second marriage with Elizabeth Lewis: 5. Robert Starkey, born Nov. 5, 1800; 6. Jane Westmoreland, born April 10, 1802.

Capt. William Armistead moved in 1819 to Clarke county, Ala., and died there in 1842. His son, Westwood, married Elizabeth Boroughs, daughter of Bryan Boroughs and Sally Waddell, in North Carolina, came to Alabama and died in 1845. His children were James W., Bryan, William W., Robert S., Emma, who married ——— Cunningham, Elizabeth, married her second cousin, John Kimbell.

The second son of Capt. William Armistead, John Kimbell, married Julia Gaines. They lived in Wilcox county, Ala., thence he moved with his family to Mississippi about 1840. Issue: William, James, Gen. Charles Armistead, of the Confederate army, John, and Dr. E. R. Armistead, of Prescott, Ala.

The third son of Capt. William Armistead, Robert Starkey, married Ann Carney, moved to Texas in 1835, and died in 1866, without issue.

The oldest daughter of William Armistead, Elizabeth Lee, married his step-son, John Morriss, and lived in Alabama; and his second daughter married Edmund Waddell of North Carolina, an uncle of Westwood Armistead's wife.

The youngest daughter of Capt. Armistead married in Alabama in 1821, Dr. Neal Smith, a native of Moore county, N. C., son of Malcolm Smith. Malcolm Smith, and Malcolm Smith, Sr., were soldiers of the Revolution and though of Scotch descent, their worst foes were the "Scotch Tories." (See Ball's *Clarke County, Ala.*, and Brewer's *Alabama* for sketches of Dr. Neal Smith.) Issue: Julia Elizabeth, married (1) David White, a native of Virginia, (2) James M. Jackson; Sarah Louisa married John B. Savage; Margaret A. married (1) Kirkland Harrison, of South Carolina, (2) Asa M. Lewis, of Texas; Robert Neal married Miss Watkins, from Virginia; Jane married James D. Bryant, of Wilcox county, Ala.; Martha Rebecca married (1) Richard Starkey Jones, of Selma, and (2) Mr. Rixey; Catharine Jeanet married Dr. H. G. Davis; Mary Caroline married Thomas Boroughs, Jr.

The Revolutionary services of Capt. William Armistead, copied from archives at Washington, D. C., Record Book E, vol 8, p. 9:

"William Armistead was born in Elizabeth City, Va., about 1762. He entered the U. S. service at Williamsburg, Va., under Captain Spiller Dent, 1777, Virginia State Troops; marched to Valley Forge, joined Muhlenburg Brigade; pursued the British on their retreat through Jersey; was in the battle of Monmouth; afterwards detached from Muhlenburg Brigade and attached to troops under command of General Wayne and Major Llewry; marched to Hudson river; stationed between West Point and Stony Point for some time; was at the storming of Stony Point, 1779. After long service marched to New Brunswick on Raritan river; remained in Philadelphia some time. After serving three years, marched back to Williamsburg, Va., and was there with the other troops regularly discharged."

William Armistead, of Clarke county, Ala., is down on the U. S. Pension List for 1840.

The following additional facts as to his family are supplied by William B. Newman, of Talladega:

John Morriss and his wife, Elizabeth Lee Armistead, had four children:

(1) William Armistead, married Nancy, a sister of the late William J. Hearin, of Mobile.

(2) Rebecca Kimbell, married Thomas Boroughs, brother of Westwood Armistead's wife.

(3) Washington.

(4) Martha Jane, married Samuel Forwood, a Marylander,

who was executor, with Westwood Armistead, of William Armistead's will.

Rebecca Kimbell Morriss had by her husband, Thomas Boroughs, the following children:

(1) Anne Elizabeth, married (1) Henley W. Coate, first judge of probate of Clarke; (2) James Addison Newman, of Orange county, Virginia.

(2) William Morriss, married Laura Jenkins, of Monroe county.

(3) Thomas, married his cousin, Mary Caroline Smith.

(4) Martha Jane, married her cousin, Captain Thomas Isham Kimbell, of Clarke.

(5) Rebecca, married Frank Stallworth, of Falls county, Texas, a native of Conecuh county, Ala.

(6) Mary Louise, died unmarried.

(7) Bryan, married Elizabeth, daughter of James Shelton Dickinson, a member of the second Confederate congress.

REUBEN BLANKENSHIP.

"Simple they were, not savage; and their rifles
Though very true were yet not used for trifles."

Reuben Blankenship is mentioned in the list of Alabama pensioners in the U. S. Census for 1840. His age then was given as seventy-three; so he was born about 1767 and was a youth during the Revolution. In 1840 he was living in Coosa county, and he was buried at Poplar Springs church in that county.

This information was given by D. B. Oden, of Childersburg, Ala.

THOMAS BRADFORD.

"The night dew that falls though in silence it weeps
Shall brighten with verdure the grass where he sleeps."
—*Thomas Moore.*

The following description of the grave of this Revolutionary soldier was copied from Rev. T. H. Ball's *Clarke County, Alabama,* p. 476. The writer has endeavored vainly by correspondence and advertisements to obtain information of the life and descendants of Mr. Bradford. Apparently he is totally forgotten by the world and "in this secluded nook where peace and quiet reign, this honored soldier sleeps his last long dreamless sleep forever." Ball says:

"Not many miles north of Amity church, on this same Choctaw line, stands the grave and memorial stone of another Revolutionary soldier.

"THOMAS BRADFORD.—A slight enclosure surrounds this lone burial spot, and the headstone, with its few and simple words, reminds every passer-by of man's mortality, and also that the dust is sleeping there of one of the soldiers of '76, the Immortal Band of whom a South Carolina patriot, and eloquent Christian lawyer, asks the touching, the thrilling question, 'Shall they meet again in the amaranthine bowers of spotless purity, of perfect bliss, of eternal glory?'

"Thomas Bradford had two sons, Brasil and Nathan."

JAMES CALDWELL,

"Green be the graves where our heroes are lying."

This Revolutionary soldier is buried in the cemetery at old Davisville, in Calhoun county, Ala., one and one-half miles south of Iron City station, twelve miles east of Anniston, on the Southern railroad. The "oldest inhabitant" could give no information concerning the soldier.

The tomb is built of brick; about 8 feet long, 6½ feet wide, and 5 feet high. The shingles of the roof are badly rotted. A plain marble tablet is let into the wall of the tomb, bearing this inscription:

Sacred
to the memory of
JAMES CALDWELL,
who died October 2nd,
1847;
in the 98th year
of his age.
He was a soldier of the Revolution.

The above account was furnished by W. B. Bowling, of Lafayette, Ala.

Efforts have been made in vain to find the history of this old soldier. It is said that he came from South Carolina. He is another one of those forgotten heroes whose graves are scattered over the State.

"To forget the heroic past, is to introduce the germ of future decay."

JERRY CHANCELLOR.

"After life's fitful fever he sleeps well."

This soldier of the Revolution is buried in a country churchyard at Pine Level Methodist church, in Autauga county, eighteen miles west of Montgomery.

A short sketch of the life of Jerry Chancellor may be found in the *Memorial Record of Alabama*, vol. ii., p. 895. He was born in England and came to America with his father and two brothers, when sixteen years of age. This was during the Revolutionary war. After remaining a short time in Virginia, the father and his two oldest sons, William and Jerry, came to South Carolina, leaving the youngest son, Jackson Chancellor, in Virginia. Tradition says that Chancellorsville, Virginia, was named for the family of this youngest son.

When the Chancellors arrived in South Carolina they found the war raging violently all around them and it became necessary for them to decide what their own course should be. The father, whose loyalty to England could not be shaken, told his sons that he should join the British; the sons declared that they admired the Americans for standing up for their rights and they intended to cast their lots with the people of their adopted country. The father and sons never met again, but fought on opposite sides until the close of the Revolutionary war. We do not know in what regiment Jerry Chancellor served, but Saffell's *Records*, p. 293, states that Nov. 1, 1779, William Chancellor was a private in the South Carolina regiment commanded by Lieut. Col. Francis Marion, Seventh Company, Thomas Dunbar, captain.

Jerry Chancellor married Galatea Gilbert and settled in South Carolina after the Revolution, where he remained until 1818, when he organized a colony in South Carolina and came with them to Alabama. They settled on the Autauga side of the Alabama river. He remained with this colony until his death. Descendants of Jerry Chancellor are now living in Childersburg and in Coosa county. His grandson, William S. Chancellor, was one of the oldest Masons in Alabama.

JAMES COLLIER.

"And who were they our fathers? In their veins
Ran the best blood of England's gentlemen,
Her bravest in the strife on battle plains,
Her wisest in the strife of voice and pen."

—*Halleck.*

James Collier, a Revolutionary soldier, is buried on his plantation near Triana, Madison county, Alabama, about twenty miles from Huntsville.

His wife is buried beside him and their monuments, with inscriptions, are now standing in a full state of preservation in the old family burying ground. The inscriptions are as follows:

To the memory of
JAMES COLLIER,
who was born in Lunenburg Co., Va., Oct. 13th,
A. D. 1757, and died the 20th of August, A. D. 1832.
"And though after my skin worms destroy this body,
yet in my flesh shall I see God: whom I shall see for
myself and my eyes shall behold and not another."

To the memory of
ELIZABETH BOULDIN,
of Charlotte Co., Va., wife of James Collier, who was
born the 13th of Feb., A. D. 1763, and died the 23d of
Feb., A. D. 1828.
"All flesh is grass, and all the goodliness thereof is as
a flower of the field, for the wind passeth over it and it
is gone and the place thereof shall know it no more."

James Collier was the son of Cornelius Collier and Elizabeth Wyatt, of Lunenburg county, Va., He was descended from Charles Collier, of King and Queen county, Va., on his father's side, and his mother was nearly related to Sir Francis Wyatt, Colonial governor of Virginia. It was the old flax wheel of his (James Collier's) cousin, Mary Collier, the ancestor of the late Prof. G. Brown Goode, which suggested the insignia of the Daughters of the American Revolution. James Collier was wounded at the battle of Eutaw Springs by a sabre cut across his cheek, in a hand-to-hand encounter with a British soldier. He killed the soldier and carried the scar on his face to his grave. His brother, Wyatt Collier, was killed at the same battle when only a boy.

James Collier married Elizabeth Bouldin, July 3, 1788, daughter of James Bouldin and Sally Watkins, of Charlotte county, Va. He was a large land owner in Lunenburg county and resided there until 1802, when he, with his little family, followed his father and other relatives to Abbeville District, South Carolina. He was a large planter in that State until 1818, when he followed his sons to the territory of Alabama, his older sons having settled in that part of the Mississippi territory, now Alabama, in 1812. He settled on a large plantation in Madison county, where he lived and died.

His wife, Elizabeth Bouldin, was the daughter of James Bouldin, who was the oldest son of Colonel Thomas Bouldin of Colonial fame, who settled in Lunenburg (now Charlotte) county, Virginia, in 1744, coming from Pennsylvania. His wife was Nancy Clark, niece of Captain Richard Wood of the English navy. This family of Bouldins are noted for their intellect and their love for the legal profession. Virginia boasts there has never been a generation without a judge, even to the present day. This couple left a large family of sons, but there were only four grandsons among the grandchildren. Governor Henry Watkins Collier was a son of James Collier. He was closely connected with the politics of Alabama from 1822 until his death in 1855.

The ancestry of James Collier is as follows:

(1) Charles Collier of King and Queen county, Virginia. One of his children,—

(2) John Collier, Sr., (1680-1735), who was married three times, by his third wife, Nancy Eyres, had issue, among others:

(3) Cornelius Collier, born 1725, married Elizabeth Wyatt in Gloucester county, Va., about 1750, lived in Lunenburg county, Va., was a soldier in the Revolution and moved to Abbeville District, South Carolina in 1788; he had four sons and one of them was—

(4) James Collier, the subject of this sketch.

The facts of this article were furnished by his great-granddaughter, Miss Elizabeth R. Benagh. James Collier is mentioned in the *Memorial Record of Alabama*, vol. ii, p. 415.

REV. ROBERT CUNNINGHAM.
"Soldier of Christ, well done!"

Rev. Robert Cunningham lies buried near the central part of the old cemetery in Tuscaloosa. A stately marble shaft marks

35

his grave; the epitaph which covers the four sides of the shaft is
in Latin, showing among other things that he had been a soldier
of the Revolution, and pastor of Presbyterian churches in Georgia
and in Lexington, Kentucky.

These inscriptions are as follows:

On the west face:

Hic Sepultus Jacet
Vir ille
Admodum reverendus
ROBERTUS M. CUNNINGHAM, D. D.
Belli Revolutionis,
Americanae miles fidelis.
etiamque
Crucis Domini Jesu Christi:

On the east face:

Ecclesiae Presb.
in Republica Georgiae
Pastor
Multos annos.
Et in urbe Lexingtonia
Rep. Kentuckiensis
Eundem honorem tulit.

On the south face:

Qui
De Religione, de Patria
Optime meritus:
Maximo suorum
et bonorum omnium
Desiderio
Mortem obiit,
Die Jul. XI: Anno Domini:
MDCCCXXXIX:
Aetatis suae
LXXX.

On the north face:

Uxor dilectissima
Hoc monumentum
ponendum
Curavit.

The facts concerning the life of this distinguished man are mostly taken from Saunders' *Early Settlers of Alabama*, p. 197. The author says that the importance of historical societies is shown from the fact that very little information could be obtained for this biography from any source until he wrote to the Presbyterian Historical Society of Philadelphia, when he promptly received a circumstantial account of the events of his life.

Robert M. Cunningham, a son of Roger and Mary Cunningham, was born in York county, Pennsylvania, September 10, 1760. In 1775 his parents removed to North Carolina. Query 293 of the Historical and Genealogical Department of the *Montgomery* (Ala.) *Advertiser* states that "Roger Cunningham and wife, —— Sturgeon, removed from near Gettysburg, Pennsylvania, to Mecklenburg county, North Carolina, just previous to the Revolutionary war. They had six children,—Robert, William, James, Nelly, Mary and Margaret." There is little room to doubt that this is the same family as that of the subject of this sketch, and that his mother's name was Mary Sturgeon.

Robert served as a youthful soldier in the North Carolina contingent during the Revolutionary war, but it is not known to what regiment he was attached. At the close of the war he went to school to the Rev. Robert Finley, Mr. Robert McCulloch and the Rev. Joseph Alexander. In 1787, being 26 years of age, he entered the junior class in Dickinson College, Carlisle, Pa., and graduated in 1789.

On leaving college he returned to his parents and taught school while he studied theology. He was licensed to preach by the First Presbytery of South Carolina in 1792. Here he married his first wife, Elizabeth, daughter of Charles and Mary Moore, of Spartanburg District. A sketch of the life of Charles Moore is given in J. B. Landrum's *History of Spartanburg*, p. 189. He was a brave and faithful old patriot. Elizabeth died November 3, 1794, leaving a daughter who died young.

In the autumn of 1792 he went to Georgia and organized a church called Ebenezer, in Hancock county; he also preached at Bethany church. October 15, 1795, he married Betsy Ann, daughter of Joseph Parks, of Prince Edward county, Virginia, and by this marriage he had five sons, one of whom was the Rev. Joseph Cunningham, a minister of ability. October 14, 1805, he married as a third wife, Emily, daughter of Col. William Bird, of Warren county, Georgia, originally from Pennsylvania, who survived him. Hers was a family of distinction.—See Dubose's *Life of Yancey*. Three of her aunts on her father's side married signers of the Declaration of Independence, James Wilson and George Ross, of Pennsylvania, and George Read, of Delaware. Her sister, Caroline Bird, married Benjamin Cudworth Yancey, and was the mother of the great Southern orator, William Lowndes Yancey. Another sister, Louisa Bird, married Capt. Robert Cunningham of "Rosemont," South Carolina, a gentleman of great wealth, liberality and high culture, and an officer in the war of 1812. Their daughter, Miss Ann Pamela Cunningham, was the founder of the Mt. Vernon Ladies' Memorial Association and was its first regent. Another sister married Jesse Beene, of Cahaba, Alabama, a distinguished lawyer and politician. A brother, Will E. Bird, was county judge of Dallas county, Alabama, 1836. It is a singular coincidence that Emily Bird married Rev. Robert Cunningham, of Georgia, and another sister, Louisa Bird, married Capt. Robert Cunningham, of South Carolina. Rev. Robert Cunningham at the time of this marriage must have won much distinction in a ministerial and social respect. By this last marriage he had a son, Robert, a physician, who died in Sumter county, Alabama, and three daughters,—Mrs. Maltby, Mrs. Wilson and Louisa.

In 1807 he removed to Lexington, Kentucky, and was installed pastor of the First Presbyterian church. This town was even then celebrated for its wealth and intellectual culture and this pulpit required a minister of learning and eloquence. He remained in Lexington until 1822, when he removed to Moulton, in North Alabama. He had been laboring as a minister for thirty years, and, requiring some relaxation, he bought a plantation but preached in Moulton and surrounding villages. In 1826 he bought a farm eleven miles from Tuscaloosa and removed there. He built up churches in Tuscaloosa and at Carthage; he also preached occasionally at Greensboro, where his son, Joseph, was pastor. For eight years he preached a free gospel at Tuscaloosa. He preached his last sermon in 1838. He received the degree of doctor of divinity from Franklin College, Georgia (now the University), in 1827. In 1836 he removed to Tuscaloosa, and he died there on the 11th of July, 1839, 80 years of age. Dr. Cunningham was a man of impressive appearance; his height was more than six feet and his form was well developed; his features were good with expressive eyes; he was a man of learning, eloquence and power in preaching; a man of charity, beloved by Christians of all denominations, and his tenderness in preaching opened many hearts. This old saint was called in Alabama "Father Cunningham"; and he is thus described in Nall's *Dead of the Synod of Alabama*: "Very few men ever exhibited more of clear and sound intellect— of tender, melting pathos—and of bold and manly eloquence—than did this patriarch of the church."

GEN. JOHN ARCHER ELMORE.

"America shall not perish but endure while the spirit of our fathers animates the sons."

Elmore county was named in honor of Gen. Elmore. He was deservedly popular for his "candor, good sense and sociability."

He was buried in the old family burying ground at the old homestead, "Huntington," in Elmore county. The following inscription is upon his tombstone:

In
Memory of
GEN. JOHN ARCHER ELMORE,
who was born in
Prince Edward County, Va.,
August the 21st, 1762,
and died in
Autauga County, Ala.,
April the 24th, 1834,
aged 71 yrs. 8 mos. & 3 days.
He was a soldier of the Revolution
in the Virginia line
and afterwards a member of the Legislature of So. Ca., and a General in
the militia.
He was a member of the Legislature of
Alabama
and filled various other offices of Honor
and Trust in both States.
He was an affectionate husband,
a kind and indulgent father,
a humane master,
a devoted friend, and
a patriot citizen.

Gen. John Archer Elmore was born in Prince Edward county, Virginia, Aug. 21, 1762, and died in Autauga county, Alabama, April 24, 1834. He entered the Revolutionary service, a mere lad, in Greene's command in the Virginia line; was with him in his tour through the Carolinas, and with him at the surrender at Yorktown. This is shown by the archives in Washington; O'Neal's *Bench and Bar of South Carolina*, vol. ii, pp. 85, 88, and Brewer's *Alabama*, p. 109. After the Revolution he settled in Laurens district, South Carolina, and resided there many years, during which time he was often a member of the legislature. He moved to Autauga county, Alabama, in 1819 and served one term in the house of representatives from this county.

His first wife was Miss Saxon, by whom he had two sons: Hon. Franklin H. Elmore, of South Carolina, who succeeded Mr. Calhoun in the United States senate, and Benjamin F. Elmore, treasurer of South Carolina. His second wife, Miss Ann Martin, was a member of the famous Martin family of South Carolina, and descended also from the Marshall family of Virginia, and from Lieutenant Nathaniel Terry, of Virginia. By this second marriage there were five sons and several daughters. One of the daughters married Gov. Benj. Fitzpatrick, another married Hon. Dixon H. Lewis of Lowndes; another married Dr. J. T. Hearne, of Lowndes, and she is still (1904) living in Montgomery. The sons were Hon. John A. Elmore, a distinguished lawyer in Montgomery; William A. Elmore, a lawyer in New Orleans since 1835, superintendent of the mint until the outbreak of the war, and who died in Philadelphia in 1891; Capt. Rush Elmore, who commanded a company in the Mexican war and was territorial judge of Kansas; Henry Elmore, who was probate judge of Macon county prior to the war, and who afterwards moved to Texas; Albert Elmore, of Montgomery, secretary of State in 1865 and collector of customs in Mobile under President Johnson.—*Memorial Record of Alabama*, vol. ii, p. 427.

THOMAS HAMILTON.

"Nor while the grass grows on the hill, and streams flow through the vale, May we forget our father's deeds or in their covenant fail."

Thomas Hamilton, one of the five children of David Hamilton and Margaret Carlisle, was born in Belfast, Ireland, April 9,

1758. Their family emigrated to America about 1762, landing in Virginia after a voyage of nearly three months. Upon their arrival, David Hamilton settled in Culpeper county, where he lived with one of his sons. Thomas Hamilton was married on the 28th of May, 1782, to Temperance Arnold, daughter of Benjamin Arnold and Ann Hendrick of South Carolina. During the Revolution, Benjamin Arnold, an old man, left South Carolina on account of the troubles resulting from the war, and carried his family for greater safety to Culpeper county, Va., where they became acquainted with Thomas Hamilton. After their marriage in 1782, they returned to the old home of Benjamin Arnold in South Carolina, where they settled upon a place between Andy creek on the east and Horse creek on the west in Greenville district. Here they lived until 1821, when they moved to Butler county, Ala., near Greenville, and remained there until 1826, when they moved to Lowndes county, ten miles south of Benton, where they both died. They are buried in Watkins cemetery, near Collirene, Lowndes county. Thomas died in August, 1844, aged 86, and his wife July 22, 1849, aged 87. The spot is marked by a marble obelisk, erected to the memory of the family. The following inscription, with no dates, is among others: "Thomas and Temperance Hamilton rest here." Thomas Hamilton was with Sumter but not in the regular army. He was at the battles of the Cowpens, Eutaw Springs and King's Mountain. He was in the brigade commanded by Colonel Campbell at the latter place. After his death in 1844, over sixty years after the Revolutionary war, few of the participants of that mighty struggle were left on earth. The citizens of Lowndes county asked permission to bury him with military honors.

This account was prepared by a descendant, Gordon Rives Catts, now a cadet at West Point. The name of Thomas Hamilton of Lowndes county, Ala., may be found in the *Census of Pensioners for 1840.*

WILLIAM HEARNE.

"There be of them that have left a name behind them that their praises might be reported."—*Ecclesiasticus.*

In the *Memorial Record of Alabama,* vol. ii, p. 426, mention is made of William Hearne from North Carolina, a Revolutionary soldier, and it states that he died in Lowndes county, Ala. The grave is in a private burying ground which is now on the plantation belonging to I. D. Hauser of Opelika. It is on that part of the plantation that he bought of the Mickle estate, and very near Manack Station. It is surrounded by a brick wall and apparently contains three or four graves.

William Hearne was a great-grandson of William Hearne of Maryland (1630), a wealthy merchant and planter. Thomas Hearne, a son of this colonist, married Sally Wingate; he had twelve children, one of them, Nehemiah, married Betty ——— and lived in Somerset county, Md. A son of Nehemiah, William Hearne, was born in Somerset county, Md., in 1746; he married his cousin, Tabitha Hearne, and moved to North Carolina, when it was a new country. At the commencement of the Revolutionary war he enlisted and served during the seven years and only missed being at General Gates' defeat at Camden by being left behind with smallpox. He came to Alabama in 1819; he died September 21, 1832, in Lowndes county, Ala. These facts are obtained from the *Hearne History,* p. 383.

He left many descendants, among them may be mentioned the late Dr. Joseph T. Hearne, physician and extensive planter of St. Clair, Lowndes county.

JACOB HOLLAND.

"Not honor they sought, nor life's shallow fame,
Nor glory, nor hope of renown."

Very little is known of this Revolutionary soldier, who came from South Carolina and is buried at Hebron churchyard, in Greene county.

The following inscription is upon his tombstone:

Sacred to the
memory of
JACOB & SARAH HOLLAND
Jacob
departed this life
Oct. 1st, 1852,
Aged 91 years.
Sarah
May 13th, 1851,
Aged 87 years.

CHARLES HOOKS.

"O few and weak their numbers were—
A handful of brave men
But to their God they gave their prayer
And rushed to battle then."

Charles Hooks is buried in Montgomery county, about twenty miles from the city of Montgomery, in a family burial ground on his plantation. It is now known as the "Old Moulton Place." His services in the Revolution in North Carolina are mentioned in Wheeler's *History of North Carolina*, and Mrs. Ellet's *Women of the Revolution*. There is an interesting chapter in the latter book, called "Mary Slocumb," which gives a delightful account of the beautiful home and patriotic deeds of Mary Hooks Slocumb, elder sister of Charles Hooks. Her husband was Lieutenant Ezekiel Slocumb, who raised a troop of light horse to watch the enemy and punish the Tories. In April, 1781, just after the battle of Guilford Court House, the British colonel, Tarleton, made his headquarters at the Slocumb home in Wayne county. Charles Hooks, a lad of thirteen at the time, was away with his brother-in-law, Lieut. Slocumb, in hot pursuit of some Tory marauders. They narrowly escaped being captured upon their return, as they were ignorant of the fact that a thousand men were in possession of their home, but the warning of a faithful slave enabled them to retreat with safety.

Charles Hooks was born in Bertie county, North Carolina, February 20th, 1768, and died in Montgomery county, Alabama, on the 18th of October, 1843. After the Revolution he married Mary Ann Hunter; she was the daughter of Isaac Hunter and Priscilla ———, and granddaughter of Isaac Hunter of Chowan, N. C., who died in 1752, and whose will is on file among the records at Edenton, N. C.

Charles Hooks became a man of distinction. He went to the legislature from Duplin county in 1802-03-04 and again in 1810-11. He served seven years as a member of Congress in 1816-17 and again from 1819 to 1825. He moved to Alabama in 1826.

The descent of Charles Hooks is as follows:

(1) William Hooks, of Chowan county, North Carolina, who died in 1751 at an advanced age. Issue: William and John.

(2) John Hooks died in 1732; his wife was Ruth ———; several children, among others,

(3) Thomas Hooks, who married (1) Anna ———, and had children Mary, Charles and one other; married (2) Mrs. John Charles Slocumb.

Many descendants of Charles Hooks are living in Alabama.

COL. JOSEPH HUGHES.

"Give them the meed they have won in the past,
Give them the honors their merits forecast."

Col. Joseph Hughes came from Union district, South Carolina, to Greene county, Alabama, in 1825. He was buried at Hebron cemetery in that county.

The inscription upon his tomb is as follows:

In memory of
COL. JOSEPH HUGHES,
who departed this life
September 4th, 1834.
Aged 85 years.

He was twice married; the name of his first wife has not been ascertained. She left seven children; their names were William, Wright, Joseph, Mary, Martha, Sarah and Jane. Col. Joseph Hughes married for a second wife, Annie Brown of South Carolina; they had three children, Stewart, James and Annie. She was an aunt of Governor Albert G. Brown, of Mississippi. Her brother, John Brown, was killed at the battle of Cowpens. All of the children of Col. Hughes came to Alabama except William, who married and settled in South Carolina, and Wright, who was captain of a steamboat on Broad river in South Carolina. Mary married ——— Kennedy; Martha, ——— Morris; Sarah, ———— Maberry; Jane, ——— Bruner; Annie, ——— White.

Col. Hughes was a consistent member of the Presbyterian church. He is well remembered by Mrs. Jay, of Benevola, Ala., who is now (1904) in her ninetieth year. She has often heard him speak of his experiences in the Revolutionary war and she has seen and handled his sword and pistol which were sacredly preserved because of their Revolutionary associations.

Some of the brave exploits of Lieut. Joseph Hughes are described in Saye's *Memoir of McJunkin;* an interesting biographical sketch of him may be found in a pamphlet entitled *The Life of Col. James D. Williams* (1898), by Rev. J. D. Bailey; and several notices of Capt. Joseph Hughes occur in Draper's *King's Mountain and its Heroes*, from which the following brief account of his life is taken, pp. 122, 129, 131-33, 277.

"He was born in what is now Chester county, South Carolina, in 1761, his parents having retired there temporarily from the present region of Union county, on account of Indian troubles. He served in 1776 on Williamson's Cherokee expedition and subsequently in Georgia. Governor Rutledge, early in 1780, commissioned him as a lieutenant and he fought under Sumter at Rocky Mount and Hanging Rock; and then shared in the heroic action of Musgrove's Mill. His dare-devil character and adventurous services in the up-country region of South Carolina during the summer and autumn of 1780 have already been related.

"Then we find him taking part in the memorable engagements at King's Mountain, Hammond's Store and Cowpens. Though yet a lieutenant, he commanded his company in this latter action. He was not only a man of great personal strength, but of remarkable fleetness on foot. As his men with others broke at the Cowpens and fled before Tarleton's cavalry; and though receiving a sabre cut across his right hand, yet with his drawn sword, he would out-run his men, and passing them, face about and command them to stand, striking right and left to enforce obedience to orders; often repeating with a loud voice: 'You d—d cowards, halt and fight,—there is more danger in running than in fighting, and if you don't stop and fight you will all be killed.'

"But most of them were for a while too demoralized to realize the situation or to obey their officers. As they would scamper off, Hughes would renewedly pursue and once more gaining their front would repeat his tactics to bring them to their duty. At length the company was induced to make a stand on the brow of a slope, some distance from the battle line behind a clump of young pines that partially concealed and protected them from Tarleton's cavalry. Others now joined them for self-protection. Their guns were loaded quickly and they were themselves again. Morgan galloped up and spoke words of encouragement to them. The next moment the British cavalry were at them; but the Whigs reserved their fire till the enemy were so near that it was terribly effective, emptying many a British saddle, when the survivors recoiled. Now Colonel Washington gave them a charge,—the bat-

tle was restored when Howard with his Marylanders with the bay-
onet, swept the field. Tarleton acknowledges that 'an unexpected
fire from the Americans, who came about as they were retreating,
stopped the British and threw them into confusion' when a panic
ensued and then a general flight. It was a high and worthy com-
pliment' from his old commander, Colonel Brandon, who declared
that at the Cowpens 'Hughes saved the fate of the day.'

"As a deserved recognition of these meritorious services he
was promoted to a captaincy early in 1781, when he was scarcely
twenty years of age and led his company with characteristic valor
at the battle of Eutaw Springs. The Tories had killed his father
during the war and many a dear friend, and his animosity against
the whole race was alike bitter and unrelenting. In 1825 he removed to Alabama, first to Greene county and then to Pickens,
where he died in September, 1834, in his seventy-fourth year.
For more than twenty of the closing years of his life he was an
elder in the Presbyterian church and the rough and almost tiger-
like partisan became as humble and submissive as a lamb. He
rose to the rank of colonel in the militia. He was tall and com-
manding in his appearance, jovial and affable in conversation; yet
his early military training rendered him to the last stern and rigid
in discipline. In all that makes up the man he was a noble speci-
men of the Revolutionary hero."

JOHN WADE KEYES.

"No lack is in your parent stock
No weakling founders builded here;
They were the men of Plymouth Rock—
The Puritan and Cavalier."

The last resting place of this Revolutionary soldier is in an old
family burial ground upon his plantation, three miles from Athens
on the Huntsville road. His lovely rural home was situated upon
a hill about half a mile from Swan creek. His wife, Louisa Talbot Keyes, lies beside him. John Wade Keyes was born in Mystic,
near Boston, Mass., Sept. 25, 1752, and died near Athens, Ala.,
Feb. 13, 1839. His ancestry and many acts of his life are told in
a book of the Keyes family called *Solomon Keyes and His Descendants*, by Judge Asa Keyes, of Vermont, published in Bat-
tleboro. We find from this that he was the son of Capt. Humphrey Keyes and Marcella Wade. His father was a sea captain of

Boston. After many successful voyages he was wrecked and taken captive by the Algerines. He was a prisoner for years, but finally made his escape. Upon his return to Boston he took John, his oldest son, and went down into Virginia. An old family record in Tennessee shows that Capt. Humphrey Keyes in 1775 was proprietor of "Keyes Ferry" on the Shenandoah river. A member of the family has now in his possession a letter written by General Washington relative to the survey of the Keyes Ferry tract on the Shenandoah near Charleston, Jefferson county, Virginia. John Wade Keyes married January 27, 1773, in Virginia, Louisa Talbot, niece of President Monroe. She was born near Alexandria, Va., April 20, 1756, and died near Athens, Nov. 6, 1836. This happy couple lived together for sixty-three years.

Early in the Revolutionary war there was a call made for volunteers under Gen. John Thomas in the Shenandoah Valley. John Wade Keyes was the second man to enlist; he was engaged in the battles of Bunker Hill, Lexington, Trenton, White Plains, Princeton, Brandywine and King's Mountain. Capt. John Keyes settled near Alexandria, Virginia, moved thence to the vicinity of Blountsville, Sullivan county, East Tennessee, and finally to Athens, Limestone county, Alabama, where he was one of the pioneer settlers. It is said that he would never consent to apply for a pension and when asked for his reasons he would reply, "I fought for patriotism, not pensions." He greatly honored and loved George Washington and he showed his admiration by naming his twin sons for him; one was called George and the other Washington. George Keyes commanded a company under Gen. Jackson and was afterwards made a brigadier-general of militia. Among the descendants of John Wade Keyes were Chancellor Wade Keyes, one of the most prominent jurists that Alabama has produced; George P. Keyes, a noted journalist; Col. John B. Richardson, of New Orleans, commander of the famous "Washington Artillery" during the war, and others of distinction at the present day.

EPHRAIM KIRBY.

"They battled for God, their country's fair name
And the flag that never came down."

Ephraim Kirby was the first Superior Court judge in what is now Alabama. He was also the first General Grand High Priest of the Royal Arch Masons of the United States, 1798-1804, and he is probably the highest ranking Mason ever buried in Alabama. Judge Kirby was the grandfather of Edmund Kirby Smith, the distinguished Confederate general. The following sketch of his life is condensed from a paper[2] read by Hon. Thomas M. Owen before the Alabama State Bar Association, June 29, 1901:

"Mr. Kirby was born Feb. 23, 1757, in Judea Society, Ancient Woodbury, Conn., and was the son of Abraham Kirby, a farmer. The house in which he was born has long since been destroyed, but the land on which it stood is still known as 'the Kirby farm.' About 1763 his parents removed to Litchfield, Conn. His boyhood days were spent in the occupation usually engaging a farmer's lad, but incidents of these years, and of his early education are wanting.

"However, he was trained as a patriot, for on the news of the battle of Lexington, he joined a company of volunteers and arrived at Boston in time to take part in the battle of Bunker Hill. In the latter part of 1776, together with other young men of Litchfield county, he united in forming a company of volunteer cavalry. The men furnished their own horses and equipment; and served about two years. The following is Mr. Kirby's record for this period of service; 'Ephraim Kirby, private, enlisted Dec. 24, 1776, of Litchfield, farmer. Stature 5 ft. 6, complexion dark, eyes dark, hair brown. Discharged Aug. 7, 1778.' His daring and bravery were conspicuous on many fields. He was in many battles and skirmishes. In the engagement at Elk river he received seven sabre cuts on the head, and was left on the field as dead. From the fearful cuts on his head he is said to have lost a portion of his brain, and he was for a long time unconscious. However, his intelligence was suddenly restored, and he at once re-entered the service of his country, continuing active until independence was achieved. At one time he was a lieutenant in a Rhode Island company. In all he is said to have been in nineteen battles and skirmishes, receiving thirteen wounds, including the sabre cuts already mentioned. These honorable evidences of service he carried with him to the grave.

---

[2] This paper was recast by Mr. Owen and published in *The New York Genealogical and Biographical Record,* vol. xxxiii, July, 1902, pp. 129-134, with a full page likeness.

"The Revolutionary War ended, with widened experience and aspiration he set about preparing himself for an enlarged sphere of usefulness. For awhile he was a student in Yale College, but he did not graduate. In 1787 his alma mater conferred upon him the degree of master of arts in recognition, doubtless, of his expanding reputation. In Litchfield resided Reynold Marvin, who before the war had been King's attorney, but who had relinquished his official station to throw himself with the cause of the colonists. Determining to embrace the profession of the law, Mr. Kirby entered the office of Mr. Marvin, and under his instruction he was soon admitted to the bar. It was at this time, having entered upon the practice, that he married Ruth Marvin, the daughter of his patron and teacher. From this time forth until his removal to the Southwest, although interested in many other matters, he practiced his profession in Litchfield. A fact is now to be noted which is of unusual interest. In 1789 he compiled and published the *Reports of Cases Adjudged in the Superior Court of the State of Connecticut, from the year 1785, to May, 1788,* which has the unique distinction of being the first volume of law reports published in America. His work indicates rare legal ability, and is still authority in the courts. Mr. Kirby the same year took the initiative in another matter of great moment. He wrote the pledge and organized the first society, having for its object the promotion of temperance, ever formed in America.

"With a view to bringing about a better condition in the Mississippi Territory, Congress by act of March 27, 1804, provided 'That there shall be appointed an additional judge for the Mississippi Territory, who shall reside at or near the Tombigbee settlement, and who shall possess and exercise, within the district of Washington, * * * the jurisdiction heretofore possessed and exercised by the Superior Court of the said Territory,' etc., which jurisdiction was made exclusive, with right of appeal, however, to the Superior Court at Natchez.

"Under this act President Thomas Jefferson, on April 6, 1804, appointed Ephraim Kirby as 'the additional judge.' His commission is as follows, the copy being supplied from the records of the secretary of state at Washington:

THOMAS JEFFERSON,

PRESIDENT OF THE UNITED STATES OF AMERICA.

To all who shall see these Presents, Greeting:

KNOW YE, That reposing special Trust and confidence in the Wisdom, Uprightness and Learning of Ephraim Kirby, of·Connecticut, and in pursuance of an Act of the Congress of the United States, passed on the twenty-seventh day of March, 1804, entitled "An Act for the appointment of an additional Judge for the Mississippi Territory, and for other purposes," I do appoint him the additional Judge for the said Territory to reside at or near the Tombigbee settlement; and do authorize and empower him to execute and fulfill the duties of that Office according to law, and to Have and to Hold the said Office with all the powers, privileges and emoluments to the same of right appertaining during his good behaviour, and to the end of the next Session of the Senate of the United States, and no longer.

In Testimony Whereof, I have caused these letters to be made Patent, and the Seal of the United States to be hereunto affixed.

GIVEN under my Hand at the City of Washington, the Sixth day of April, in the year of our Lord one thousand [SEAL.] eight hundred and four, and of the Independence of the United States of America, the Twenty Eighth.

TH. JEFFERSON.

By the President:
JAMES MADISON,
      Secretary of State.

"At best Judge Kirby could not have held more than one term of court, for he died on Oct. 20, 1804, at Fort Stoddert. As the U. S. government maintained a cantonment there, with a body of soldiers, his remains were interred with all the honors of war and other demonstrations of respect. His body was laid away in the little cemetery to await the last judgment. Mt. Vernon, as is known, is now in the hands of the Alabama Insane Hospitals. One of the trustees of this institution, Col. Sam'l Will John, on being told by the.writer, some months ago, of his discoveries as to Judge Kirby, made local inquiry at Mt. Vernon in reference to the matter. In response a communication was received by him from Thomas Rogers, of Mt. Vernon, from which the following pertinent extract is made:

" 'I arrived in Mt. Vernon Jan. 14, 1850. When I came here I visited Fort Stoddert. I found the remains of chimneys, which were built of sand rock; they have since been removed by negroes.

I also found broken delf, and the neck of champagne bottles.   In the cemetery, a little north of Fort Stoddert, on the lake, I found a red cedar board, at the head of a grave, with the name nicely cut, "Ephraim Kirby, died Oct. 4th, [20] 1804." * * * This board was the only one left to show where the cemetery was.   I afterwards visited the place, and found that the board had been destroyed by forest fires.'   And so it is that there is now no monument to mark the grave; and indeed the exact location of the grave will be hard to identify.

"In conclusion I think it may with all propriety be claimed that Alabama has a part in the splendid heritage left by this distinguished man.   Certainly there is in his life much to emulate. Strong of mind and will, patriotic in all crises, far-seeing and constructive in his mental operations, he towers above scores of his public contemporaries, as does the mountain peak above the hill. He was essentially a pioneer—the first to edit a published volume of official decisions and reports, the founder of the first organized temperance movement in America, and the first Superior Court judge in what is now Alabama.   An old lawyer of Litchfield pays this warm tribute to his worth: 'Colonel Kirby was a man of the highest moral as well as physical courage, devoted in his feelings and aspirations, warm, generous, and constant in his attachments, and of indomitable energy.   He was withal gentle and winning in his manners, kindly in his disposition, and naturally of an ardent and cheerful temperament, though the last few years of his life were saddened by heavy pecuniary misfortunes.   As a lawyer he was remarkable for frankness and downright honesty to his clients, striving to prevent litigation and effecting compromises. He enjoyed the friendship of many of the sages of the Revolution.' "

DAVID LINDSAY.

"No matter whence they came,
Dear is their lifeless clay—
Whether unknown or known to fame,
Their cause and country were the same."

—*Father Ryan.*

This soldier lies buried at Elliottsville, Shelby county.   This fact was furnished by D. B. Oden, of Childersburg, Ala., and the writer has been unable to learn anything more.

36

CHARLES LITTLETON.

"Though the patriot's form to earth be given
He lives in deeds which ever point to Heaven."

This soldier was from Maryland or Virginia. He rests in a little country graveyard, fifteen miles from Florence, in Lauderdale county, Alabama. This graveyard is nearly a mile from Bethel Grove Methodist church; the church being on Middle Cypress creek. He drew a pension and his grave is marked by a stone which bears this inscription:

CHARLES LITTLETON.
Revolutionary Soldier.
Died March 29th, 1848, at 3 o'clock P. M.
Aged about 103 or 105 years.

A descendant gives information that Charles Littleton was the son of Solomon Littleton, an Englishman, who owned land at or near Washington City, and is said to have built the first house on the site of Washington. He joined the rebellious colonists and, in revenge, the English captured him and placed him in a smallpox hospital at Ninety-Six, South Carolina, and thus took his life.

THOMAS LOFTON.

"He sleeps. No pompous pile marks where;
No lines his deeds describe."

This soldier came from Pendleton district, South Carolina, to Alabama. The young people of his neighborhood knew him as "Grandsire Lofton" and loved him for his kind and genial disposition; some are still living who remember his interesting stories of the Revolution. He was a member of the Presbyterian church. He is buried at Bethesda church near Benevola; no stone marks the last resting place of "Grandsire Lofton."

JAMES McCRORY.

"O Spirit of that early day
So pure and strong and true
Be with us in the narrow way
Our faithful fathers knew."

James McCrory is buried in a cemetery at "Old Bethany Church" (Primitive Baptist), near the town of Vienna in Pickens county. The following inscription is on his tombstone:

In Memory of
JAMES M'CRORY.
Died Nov. 24th, 1840, aged 82 years,
6 mo. and 9 days.
Deceased was a soldier of the Revolution and was at the
battles of Germantown, Brandywine and Guilford
Courthouse, and was one of Washington's life-
guard at Valley Forge and served his country faithfully during the war.
Peace to the soldier's dust.

He is remembered as a worthy man and upright citizen. His
descendants have not been located. In the *U. S. Census of Pensioners* for 1840 he is described as living with Robert McCrory,
probably a son.

The following account of him is copied from the *Tuscaloosa
Flag of the Union,* December, 1840:

James McCrory was born May 15, 1758, at Larga, on the river
Bann, in the county Antrim, Ireland. He sailed from Belfast in
1775 when he was 17 years old and landed at Baltimore July 1st,
in the same year. In 1776 he settled in Guilford county, N. C.,
and enlisted in the Continental army in the same year. He was
at the battle of Brandywine, September 11, 1777, under General
Washington at the battle of Germantown, and wintered at Valley
Forge in 1777-78. Subsequently he fought under General Greene
at Guilford Court House, March 15, 1781, was in the battle of
Eutaw Springs, and in the battle of Stono. He was with General
Gates at his defeat at Camden and with General Morgan in the
glorious victory at the Cowpens. For courage, good service and
meritorious conduct he was promoted to the rank of ensign in the
Life Guard of General Washington, and while acting in this ca-
pacity, he was taken prisoner and confined on board a prison ship
for six months. He came to Alabama while it was yet a territory,
and made his home at Tuscaloosa for the last twenty-five years of
his life. This true patriot died November 24, 1840, at the age of
eighty-two.

There is a list of North Carolina Continental troops published
in the *N. C. Historical and Genealogical Register,* on p. 424 of
which we find the name of James McCrory, ensign in the Ninth
regiment, under Col. John P. Williams, May 2, 1777. Thomas
McCrory was a captain in the same regiment. The services of
James McCrory are also stated in the proceedings of the 27th Con-

gress, 2d Session, in the Senate, February 4th, 1842, report of the Committee on Revolutionary Claims:

"James McCrory was a sergeant in Capt. Cook's company of the 9th regiment, enlisted on the 15th day of April, 1776, for the term of three years; on the 2d of May, 1777, he was promoted to the rank of ensign. In January, 1778, the nine regiments which composed the line, being reduced to three, the supernumerary officers were sent home, of which he was one. He then joined the nine months' men and marched to the south and was at the battle of Stono, the 30th of June, 1779, and was at Gates' defeat in August, 1780, and was taken prisoner on the 24th of February, 1781, by Tarleton's dragoons and was kept prisoner four months at Wilmington and then paroled; and in November, 1782, he took prisoner Colonel Bryant, a British officer, and gave him up to a regular officer of the American army."

In spite of this array of gallant services the committee reported adversely because of some technicality; but as the old hero had then been dead two years he was probably not very deeply affected or disappointed by the decision.

DAVID MURRAY.

"They gave us freedom to be free
We give them immortality."

This Revolutionary soldier is buried in Talladega county. The tombstone bears the following inscription:

To the memory of
DAVID MURRAY,
a Revolutionary soldier, who
departed this life 8th day
November, 1840, in the 80th
year of his age.

David Murray was born in 1760; served in the Revolutionary War, and came from Prince Edward county, Virginia, just after the war and settled in Wilkes county, Georgia. He left several children, among others Hon. Thomas W. Murray, the oldest son, who was born in Lincoln county, Ga., in 1790, and became a man of distinction, being a candidate for Congress when he died. Murray county, Georgia, is named in honor of him.—White's *Statistics of Georgia.*

It is shown by the records in Washington, D. C., that one David

Murray served as a private in Captain Satterlee's company, Colonel Moses Hazen's regiment, Continental troops, Revolutionary War. He enlisted December 30, 1776; was taken prisoner August 27, ——, and returned to his company August 4, 1779. His name last appears as that of a private on a roll, not dated, "of Persons in the Congress' Own Regt. commanded by Col. Moses Hazen, Brig. Genl. by Brevet in the service of the U. S., 1783," with remarks: "When commissioned or enlisted, 30 Dec., 1776; How Long to serve, War, 1 year; Discharged by Commander-in-Chief at close of war, 17 June, 1783."

HARRISON NICHOLSON.

"The soldier's warfare all is done
Life's wandering marches o'er."

The grave of this soldier is in the cemetery in Tuskegee. This is the inscription upon his monument:

In memory of
HARRISON NICHOLSON
A Revolutionary Soldier,
Who was born on the 12th
day of March, A. D. 1760,
and departed this life
on the 28th day of June, 1841,
Aged 81 years, 3 months,
and 16 days.

The descendants of Harrison Nicholson do not know where he was born or what State claimed him as a soldier during the Revolution. He came from Georgia, near Milledgeville, to Macon county, Ala. He married Lucinda Long Dec. 30, 1783. He died in Macon county at the home of his grandson, James Monroe Nicholson. According to the recollection of his granddaughter, Mrs. E. A. Wilkinson, he had only three sons:

(1) Britton Nicholson lived to mature years, but never married.

(2) Nathaniel Nicholson married and raised a family; he lived in Georgia in the vicinity of Milledgeville on his plantation.

(3) James Nicholson, born March 18, 1785, married Mary M. Stone, October 7th, 1813; children: 1. Mathew H. Nicholson, born Jan. 7th, 1815, married Miss H. E. Savory, December 9th,

1839, in Mexico, lived there for several years, then moved to Texas, California and to Central America, where he died. His children are now living around Chapel Hill, Texas; 2. Washington B. Nicholson, born June 28, 1818, married in Macon county, Alabama, to Miss Wafer, later moved to Claiborne Parish, Louisiana, died there in 1901. His family now live around Baton Rouge; he was the father of Col. James Nicholson, former president of the University of Louisiana at Baton Rouge; 3. Elizabeth Ann Nicholson, born October 25, 1829, married B. R. Taylor, December, 1836; he died leaving one child, Mrs. E. A. Hall, of Autaugaville. She married a second time J. B. Wilkinson, January 12, 1843, by this marriage were born nine children; 4. Lucinda Long Nicholson, born January 23, 1823, married Leonidas Howard and lived at Mulberry, Autauga county, Alabama; there were two living sons and one daughter by this marriage; 5. James Monroe Nicholson, born December 12, 1825, married Rebecca Slaton, children died, second marriage no children, third marriage in Texas, where he is still living near Chapel Hill; 6. Absalom H. Nicholson, born August 30, 1837, never married, was physician, moved to Louisiana, but died in Macon county, Alabama, 1855; and 7. John Wesley Nicholson, born October 2, 1829, died unmarried in 1851, near Autaugaville, had just graduated from Emory College, Georgia.

THOMAS OLIVER.
"Soldier, rest! thy warfare o'er."

The writer has been told that the grave of this soldier may be seen near one of the public roads about six miles from Montgomery. His tombstone relates that he was in the War of the Revolution from Culpeper county, Virginia; he was at King's Mountain and Yorktown. He died in 182-- in Montgomery county, Alabama. Nothing more has been learned of his history or family.

WILLIAM PULLEN.
"Few, few were they whose swords of old
Won the fair land in which we dwell,
But we are many, we who hold
The grim resolve to guard it well."

The grave of William Pullen is in Jefferson county, in the suburbs of Birmingham, in an old family burying ground about fifty yards from the Avondale car line between 34th and 35th streets. For many years this old graveyard was as isolated and secluded as if situated in the heart of a lonely forest, but, in the last year or two, houses have been built up thickly around it and are encroaching upon its boundaries. The grave of the soldier lies at the foot of a large oak tree; it is a rough mound of brown stones with a flat tablet topping them which bears this inscription:

Sacred to the
Memory of
WILLIAM PULLEN
A Soldier of the
Revolution,
Who died April 4th, 1845,
Aged 87 years.

His wife lies at his feet but the lettering of the tablet at her grave is illegible, only the words "Wife of William Pullen."

Descendants of William Pullen declare that he died at the age of ninety-six and that he was born in the year 1749. But as his name is found in the *Census of Pensioners* for 1840 and he is recorded as being eighty-two years of age at that date, and this agrees perfectly with what appears to be the age on the tombstone, the writer has accepted the latter as correct. William Pullen then was born in Virginia in 1758, on the Appomattox river near Petersburg. He entered the Revolutionary War from Virginia and was in service for seven years. Soon after the Revolution he moved to South Carolina and in 1820 he came to Alabama and settled near Birmingham. He was the first man buried with military honors in Jefferson county.

He left six children:

(1) Clarissa, who married Jesse Hickman, and they were the parents of W. P. Hickman, formerly county commissioner for Jefferson county.

(2) Sarah, who married James Rowan, and they were the parents of Peyton Rowan, of Jacksonville, Ala.

(3) William, married Nancy Brooks.

(4) Martha, married Joseph Hickman.

(5) Mary, married Samuel Rowan.

(6) Elizabeth, married Richard Tankersley.

It is shown in the records at Washington, D. C., in the Record and Pension Office, "that one William Pullen served as a private in Captain George Lambert's company of Continental regulars of the 14th battalion, 14th Virginia regiment of foot, commanded by Colonel Charles Lewis, Revolutionary War. He enlisted January 1, 1777, to serve three years, and his name last appears as that of a private on a roll dated Camp near Morristown, December 9, 1779, of Captain Overton's company, 10th Virginia regiment, commanded by Col. William Davies. The records show that the 14th Virginia regiment became the 10th Virginia regiment about November, 1778, and that about May, 1779, the 1st and 10th Virginia regiments were incorporated and designated the 1st and 10th Virginia regiment."

JAMES ROBERTSON.

The following tribute to "Horseshoe Robinson" is extracted from a poem, entitled "The Day of Freedom," by Alexander B. Meek, and delivered as an oration at Tuscaloosa on the 4th of July, 1838:

"Valorously
He bore himself, and with his youthful arms
Chivalrous deeds performed, which in a land
Of legendary lore had placed his name,
Embalmed in song, beside the hallowed ones
Of Douglass and of Percy; not unsung
Entirely his fame. Romance has wreathed
With flowering fingers, and with wizard art
That hangs the votive chaplet on the heart,
His story, mid her fictions, and hath given
His name and deeds to after times. When last
This trophied anniversary came round
And called Columbia's patriot children out
To greet its advent, the old man was here,
Serenely smiling as the autumn sun
Just dripping down the golden west to seek
His evening couch. Few months agone I saw
Him in his quiet home, with all around
Its wishes could demand—and by his side
The loved companion of his youthful years—
This singing maiden of his boyhood's time;
She who had cheered him with her smiles when clouds
Were o'er his country's prospects; who had trod
In sun and shade, life's devious path with him,
And whom kind Heaven had still preserved to bless,
With all the fullness of maternal wealth,
The mellowing-afternoon of his decline.
Where are they now?—the old man and his wife?
Alas! the broadening sun sets in the night,
The ripening shock falls on the reaper's arm;

The lingering guest must leave the hall at last;
The music ceases when the feast is done;
The old man and his wife are gone.　From earth,
Have passed in peace to heaven; and summer's flowers,
Beneath the light of this triumphant day,
Luxurious sweets are shedding o'er
The unsculptured grave of 'Horseshoe Robinson.' "

The grave of James Robertson is in Tuscaloosa county on the banks of the Black Warrior river near Sanders' ferry, in the old family burying-ground. He was the famous "Horseshoe Robinson" of Revolutionary fame in South Carolina, and the hero of the novel of that name written by John Pendleton Kennedy in 1835. The name "Horseshoe" was given because of a bend in a creek in his plantation in South Carolina shaped like a horseshoe.

The following inscription is taken from his tombstone:

MAJOR JAMES ROBERTSON.
A native of S. C.
died April 26, 1838, aged 79 years,
and was buried here.
Well known as Horseshoe Robinson, he earned a
just fame in the war for independence, in
which he was eminent in courage, patriotism
and suffering.　He lived fifty-six years with
his worthy partner, useful and respected, and
died in hopes of a blessed immortality.　His
children erect this monument as a tribute
justly due a good husband, father, neighbor,
patriot and soldier.

James Robertson was born in 1759; and his epitaph states that he was a native of South Carolina. He was married in 1782 and "lived fifty-six years with his worthy partner;" she died in January, 1838, and he died April 26, 1838. The name of his wife was Sarah Morris ———; tradition says her maiden name was Hayden; they left several children, one daughter was living in Mississippi a few years ago. James Robertson was a famous scout during the Revolution and a terror to the Tories. After the war he settled in Pendleton district and was living there when Kennedy met him in 1818. In the preface to Kennedy's novel of *Horseshoe Robinson* he gives an account of the circumstances which led him to write the story.

He says that in the winter of 1818-19 he had occasion to visit the western section of South Carolina. He went from Augusta to Edgefield, then to Abbeville and thence to Pendleton, in the old district of Ninety-six, just at the foot of the mountains. His course was still westward until he came to the Seneca river, a tributary of the Savannah. He describes how he happened to spend the night at the home of Col. T——, who lived thirty miles from Pendleton. Horseshoe Robinson came there that night. "What a man I saw! Tall, broad, brawny and erect. His homely dress, his free stride, his face radiant with kindness, the natural gracefulness of his motions, all afforded a ready index to his character. It was evident he was a man to confide in."

The old soldier was drawn out to relate some stories of the war. He told how he got away from Charleston after the surrender, and how he took five Scotchmen prisoners, and these two famous passages are faithfully preserved in the narrative.

"It was first published in 1835. Horseshoe Robinson was then a very old man. He had removed to Alabama and lived, I am told, near Tuscaloosa. I commissioned a friend to send him a copy of the book. The report brought me was that the old man had listened very attentively to the reading of it and took great interest in it.

"'What do you say to all this?' was the question addressed to him, after the reading was finished. His reply is a voucher, which I desire to preserve: 'It is all true and right—in its right place—excepting about them women, which I disremember. That mought be true, too; but my memory is treacherous—I disremember.'"

It is a pleasure to know that this fine old hero was a real personage, and although his exploits may have been colored in a measure by the pen of the romancer, there still remains a rich stock of adventures, which were undoubtedly true, and the picture of a nature frank, brave, true and yet full of modesty.

Extract from *Flag of the Union*, published at Tuscaloosa, January 17, 1838:

Horseshoe Robinson—Who has not read Kennedy's delightful novel of this name, and who that has read it would not give an half day's ride to see the venerable living Hero of this Tale of "Tory Ascendency," the immortal Horseshoe himself—the extermination of "Jim Curry" and Hugh Habershaw? The venerable Patriot bearing the familiar sobriquet, and whose name Mr. Kennedy has made as familiar in the mouths of American youths as household words, was visited by us in company with several friends one day last week. We found the old Gentleman on his Plantation about 12 miles from this city, as comfortably situated with respect to this world's goods as any one could desire to have him. It was gratifying to us to see him in his old age after having served through the whole war of Independence thus seated under his own vine and fig tree, with his children around him and with the Partner of his early toils and trials still continued to him enjoying in peace and safety the rich rewards of that arduous struggle, in the most gloomy and desponding hour of which he was found as ready, as earnest, as zealous, for the cause of liberty as when victory perched upon her standard, and the stars of the "Tory ascendency" was for a while dimmed by defeat—and in which he continued with unshaken Faith and constancy until it sank below the Horison never again to rise. The old gentleman gave us a partial history of his Revolutionary adventures, containing many interesting facts respecting the domination of the Tory party in the South during the times of the Revolution, which Mr. Kennedy has not recorded in his Book. But it will chiefly interest our readers, or that portion of them at least to whom the history of the old hero's achievements as recorded by Mr. Kennedy is familiar, to be assured that the principal incidents therein portrayed are strictly true.

That of his escape from Charleston after the capture of that city, his being entrusted with a letter to Butler, the scene at Wat Adair's, the capture of Butler at Grindal's Ford, his subsequent escape and recapture, the death of John Ramsey, and the detection of the party by reason of the salute fired over his grave, his capturing of the four men under the command of the younger St. Jermyn, his attack upon Ines' camp, and the death of Hugh Habershaw by his own hand and finally the death of Jim Curry, are all narrated pretty much as they occurred, in the old veteran's own language: "There is a heap of truth in it, though the writer has mightily furnished it up." That the names of Butler, Mildred Lindsay, Mary Musgrove, John Ramsay, Hugh Habershaw, Jim Curry and in fact all most every other used in the Book, with the exception of his own, are real and not fictitious. His own name, he informed us, is James; and that he did not go by the familiar appellation by which he is now so widely known until after the war, when he acquired it from the form of his Plantation in the Horseshoe Bend of the Fair Forest creek, which was bestowed upon him by the Legislature of South Carolina in consequence of the services he had rendered during the war—this estate, we understood him to say, he still owned.

He was born, he says, in 1759 in Virginia, and entered the army in his seventeenth year. Before the close of war, he says, he commanded a troop of horse, so that his military title is that of Captain. Horseshoe, although in infirm health bears evident marks of having been a man of great personal strength and activity. He is now afflicted with a troublesome cough, which in the natural course of events must in a few years wear out his aged frame. Yet, notwithstanding his infirmities and general debility, his eye still sparkles with the fire of youth, as he recounts the stirring and thrilling incidents of the war, and that sly, quiet humor so well described by Kennedy may still be seen playing around his mouth as one calls to his recollections any of the pranks he was wont to play upon any of the "tory vagrants," as he very properly styles them. The old Gentleman received us with warm cordiality and hospitality; and after partaking of the Bounties of his board and spending a night under his hospitable roof we took leave of him, sincerely wishing him many years of the peaceful enjoyment of that liberty which he fought so long and so bravely to achieve. It will not be uninteresting, we hope, to remark that the old hero still considers himself a soldier, though the nature of his warfare is changed; he is now a zealous promoter of the Redeemer's cause as he once was in securing the independence of his country.

Since the above was in type we have heard of the death of the aged partner of this venerable patriot. An obituary notice will be found in another column.

The novel *Horseshoe Robinson* is interesting reading even in this critical and blasé twentieth century. Judge A. B. Meek, a fine literary critic, says that "Mr. Kennedy, the author of 'Horseshoe Robinson,' has in that inimitable 'Tale of the Tory Ascendency' in South Carolina proved the suitableness of American subjects for fictitious composition of the most elevated kind. Although in his incidents and characters he has done little more than presented a faithful chronicle of facts, using throughout the veritable names of persons and places as they were stated to him by his hero himself, yet such is the thrilling interest of the story, the vivid pictures of scenery, manners, customs, and language, the striking contrasts of characters and the pervading beauty and power of style and description throughout the work, that we think we do not err in saying that it is not inferior in any respect to the best of the Waverly series."

The home of James Robertson in South Carolina, where he lived for a third of a century, is still standing. It is in Oconee county a few miles from Westminster. It is now owned by a Mr. Cox and travelers frequently visit the place, drawn thither by the fame of "Horseshoe Robinson."

GOVERNOR JOHN SEVIER.

"They carved not a line, they raised not a stone,
But left him alone in his glory."

This hero of the Revolution, whose life was a romance, was not one of the pioneer settlers of Alabama. He died in this State and his remains lay buried here for seventy-three years "without a stone to mark the place of their repose or an enclosure to protect them from unhallowed intrusion." In 1888 his body was removed by the State of Tennessee and laid to rest beneath the sod of the State he had loved and served so faithfully. He is now buried in Knoxville, and the State has erected a stately monument as a memorial of her everlasting though tardy gratitude to her honored son.

Valentine Xavier, the father of John Sevier, was a descendant from an ancient Huguenot family in Navarre; he was born in London and emigrated to America about 1740; settled on the Shenandoah, Virginia; removed thence to Watauga, N. C., and finally settled on the Nola Chucka, at Plum Grove.—See *Pioneer Women of the West.*

John Sevier was born in Rockingham Co., Va., 23rd of September, 1745, and was educated at the academy in Fredericksburg. He was married at the early age of seventeen to Sarah Hawkins; soon afterwards he founded Newmarket, in the valley of the Shenandoah; he became at once celebrated as an Indian fighter, and was made captain of the Virginia line in 1772. That spring (1772) he removed to Watauga, now Tennessee, served in Lord Dunmore's war and was in the battle of Point Pleasant, 1774. "His work began at the dawn of the Revolution and lasted to the end." It is said he was in thirty battles. His wife's health was delicate and she never removed from Virginia, but died in 1779, leaving him ten children. In 1780, he married Catharine Sherrill, daughter of Samuel Sherrill of North Carolina, who was one of the pioneers in the valley of the Watauga. She was beautiful, tall, strong and courageous as became the wife of John Sevier. She always boasted that the first work she did after she was married was to spin and weave and make the suits of clothes which her husband and his three sons wore in the memorable battle of King's Mountain. She became the mother of eight children, three sons and five daughters. After the battle of King's Mountain, John Sevier received a vote of thanks and a present of a sword and pistol from the North Carolina legislature. A fellow soldier said of his appearance during the battle: "His eyes were flames of fire, and his words were electric bolts crashing down the ranks of the enemy."

He was elected governor of the State of Franklin in 1784; but, as this State was not long allowed existence, Sevier was captured and imprisoned because of alleged disloyalty. However, he was rescued and soon made his escape. That section of country was then given the name by the United States government of "Territory south of the river Ohio," and he was made brigadier-general of this section in 1789. He was the first delegate sent to represent the Territory in Congress in 1790. During all this time he was incessantly and successfully engaged in defending the settlements from the Indians until their spirit was broken and peace was fully established. No man was ever more feared or respected by them, and as for the white people of the settlements, they loved him as a father, friend and protector. When the State of Tennessee was established he was elected the first governor in 1796, and served three terms. In 1815, in spite of his age and infirmities, he was appointed by President Monroe to act as United States commissioner to settle the boundary line between Georgia and the Creek territory in Alabama. He died while engaged in this work, September 24th, 1815. He was attended during his illness by only a few soldiers and Indians. He was buried near Fort Decatur, Alabama, on the east side of the Tallapoosa river, at an Indian village called Tuckabatchee, with the honors of war by the troops under command of Capt. Walker, United States army. He was in the active service of his country from a boy of eighteen until he died at the age of seventy.

A handsome monument was erected to his memory in the city of Nashville by an ardent and patriotic admirer; but his lonely grave in Alabama remained unprotected and unmarked for more than seventy years.

GEORGE TAYLOR.

"Ye, who boast
In your free veins the blood of sires like these,
Lose not their lineaments."

—*Sigourney.*

This Revolutionary soldier is mentioned in *Northern Alabama Illustrated*, p. 261. He is buried ten miles east of Huntsville, near the bank of the Flint river; there is no tombstone over his grave. Family records give the facts of his history. George Taylor was born in Virginia, exact date not known but about 1762, and died in Madison county, Alabama, 1826. He entered the Revolutionary army in his seventeenth year, was first under fire at the battle of Monmouth, 1778, then came to South Carolina with "Light Horse Harry" Lee's command and engaged in many battles and skirmishes with Lee, and at the close of the war he was a lieutenant. "He was in the disastrous charge at King's Bridge, where, owing to misdirection of orders, the advance was not supported and out of twenty, only five made good their retreat." Soon after the Revolution he married Miss Jennings, of Lexington, Oglethorpe county, Georgia, and she was probably born in Lexington. Miles Jennings, a famous Indian fighter, who is described in White's *Historical Collections of Georgia,* and who lived in Oglethorpe county, is perhaps of the same family as the wife of George Taylor. It is stated that George Taylor commanded a scouting party for defense against the Indians, for more than ten years after the close of the Revolutionary War; this party being organized at Lexington, Georgia. He was also captain in the militia. He moved from Georgia to Winchester, Tenn., in 1805, and came to Madison county, Ala., in 1810, and settled on the banks of the Flint river, where he is buried. His wife died in Alabama several years before his death. He died in 1826. A grandson of this couple was the late Judge Thomas J. Taylor, of Huntsville, probate judge of Madison county. The inherited courageous and patriotic spirit of the family is shown by the fact that Judge Taylor and six brothers were gallant soldiers and officers in the Confederate States army. A great-grandson, Douglass Taylor, is now living in Huntsville, and other descendants are living in Louisiana.

WILLIAMS TRUITT.

"A grave that lies so lone,
Without a name, without a stone."
—*Father Ryan.*

Williams Truitt lies buried at Teller's ferry on Lynch's creek. His daughter married William Chancellor, son of Jerry Chancellor, who has been already mentioned. The Chancellors of Coosa county are descendants.

These facts were furnished by D. B. Oden, Childersburg, Ala.

JOHN WEBSTER.

"And some there be which have no memorial. With their seed shall continually remain a good inheritance."—*Ecclesiasticus.*

John Webster was born in Caroline county, Va., in 1743. Early in the struggle for independence he enlisted in the Continental army and served under General Washington. He was with the American army at Yorktown, and witnessed the surrender. of Cornwallis. In 1817 he came to Alabama and during the last ten years of his life he lived in Tuscaloosa with his son, John J. Webster. He died in Tuscaloosa, September 6, 1839, in the 97th year of his age.—See Tuscaloosa *Flag of the Union,* September 14, 1839.

It is shown by the records in Washington, D. C., that one John Webster served as a private in Captain Alexander S. Dandridge's troop, 1st regiment of Light Dragoons, commanded by Colonel Bland, Continental troops, Revolutionary War. He was "appointed" July 20, 1777, to serve until December 1, 1778, and his name last appears on a pay roll for the month of November, 1778. It is also shown by the records that one John Webster served as a private in Captain Thomas Pry's company in a regiment of foot commanded by Colonel Moses Hazen, Continental troops, Revolutionary War. He enlisted April 16, 1777, to serve during the war; joined the company June 17, 1777, and his name last appears on an account covering the period from June 1 to July 31, 1779.

It is further shown by the records that one John Webster served as a carpenter in Captain Low's company, Corps of Artificers, Continental troops, Revolutionary War. He enlisted April 3, 1777, to serve to January 1, 1778, and his name last appears as that of a clerk on the roll for the period from August 3 to November 27, 1778, with remark, "Appointed September 1, 1778."

It is hardly probable that these are one and the same individual.

ROBERT WESTON.

"Their deeds of fame reviewed
Bankrupt a nation's gratitude."

Robert Weston, a soldier from North Carolina, is buried at "Shady Grove," Sumter county, Ala. His tomb records simply his birth and death and "A Revolutionary Soldier." A few brief facts of his history have been furnished by Mrs. M. C. Carpenter, his granddaughter, of Eutaw, Ala. Robert Weston was born in England, August 29, 1763, and died in Sumter county, Alabama, July 21, 1845, aged 81 years, 5 months and 8 days.

He came to America when a mere lad, with his two brothers, Isaac and Frank Weston. Although very young, he fought in the Revolution in North Carolina; was brave and quick-witted; was captured three times and sentenced to death, but made his escape each time through shrewd ability in disguising himself. He married Mary Ogilvie of South Carolina, who was born June 26, 1769, and died January 11, 1845, aged 75 years, 5 months and 15 days. The young couple settled in Fairfield district, S. C., where they resided until their children were grown. They had a large family and many descendants are still living in South Carolina, Alabama, Mississippi and Texas. One son, I. M. Weston, settled in Columbia, S. C., but the other children all removed to Alabama. Naturally the old couple followed their children and came to Sumter county, Ala., in 1833, where they purchased a home near their children and spent their old age in peace and contentment surrounded by children and grandchildren. Robert Weston was a man of intelligence and excellent education and his grandchildren remember him with the deepest affection and respect. His thrilling stories of Revolutionary times are yet remembered and told in the family.

CAPT. ANTHONY WINSTON.

"The riches of the Commonwealth
Are free strong minds and hearts of health,
And more to her than golden gain,
The cunning hand and cultured brain."

Captain Anthony Winston, of Hanover county, Virginia, a member of the Virginia convention of 1775, and a gallant captain in the Revolutionary army, lies buried in the old Winston family burying ground just out of Sheffield, Alabama. Vol. xiii, Daughters of the American Revolution *Lineage Book,* states that Anthony Winston was born in Hanover county, Virginia in 1750, married Keziah Jones and died in Alabama in 1828. He was a delegate from Buckingham county to the convention of 1775; he

37

afterwards served in the militia and rose to the rank of captain. Brewer's *Alabama* says that "he was a colonial officer of 1776 and the owner of the celebrated Portuguese giant, Peter Francisco. Capt. Winston removed first to Tennessee and subsequently settled in Madison county, Alabama, about the year 1810. He was a man of marked and elevated character." He died in 1828. He left seven sons, Anthony, John J., William, Joel W., Isaac, Edmund and Thomas J., and two daughters, Mrs. John Pettus (Alice T.) and Mrs. Jesse Jones. Capt. Winston was nearly related to Patrick Henry (a first cousin) and distinction is hereditary in the Winston family. He has many honored descendants; one of his grandsons was Governor John Anthony Winston of Sumter, the "first native born governor of Alabama." Another grandson is General Edmund Winston Pettus, now senator in the United States Congress. Another distinguished grandson was the brother of Gen. Pettus, Governor John J. Pettus, the war governor of Mississippi. Other descendants of Capt. Anthony Winston are scattered all over the Southwest, filling honorable positions with credit.

The ancestry of Capt. Winston is thus given:

Slaughter's *St. Mark's Parish* states that Isaac Winston, the most remote ancestor, was born in Yorkshire, England, in 1620. A grandson of his pursued his fortunes in Wales, where he had a large family. Three of his sons emigrated to America, and settled near Richmond, Va., in 1704. Their names were William, Isaac and James. Anthony Winston was descended from Isaac.

(1) Isaac Winston, the emigrant, married Mary Dabney and died in Hanover county in 1760, leaving six children, William, Isaac, Anthony, Lucy, Mary Ann and Sarah. Sarah was the mother of Patrick Henry.

(2) Anthony Winston (son of Isaac) married Alice, daughter of Col. James Taylor of Caroline; issue: Sarah, died single; Capt. Anthony Winston; Alice, married Judge Edmund Winston; Mary.

We are indebted to Gen. Edmund Pettus, of the United States Senate, for the following facts, and a copy of the inscription upon the tombstone:

Sacred to the memory
of
Anthony Winston and Keziah his wife,
He
Was born on the 15th of Nov. 1750
She
On the 10th of Feb. 1760.
They
Were married on the 11th of Mar. 1776
She
Died October 1826 and he in 1828

———(*   )———

This tribute of respect
Is
Paid to the memory of the best of parents
By
Their grateful
and
Affectionate sons.

They were buried at the family burying-ground on the plantation of their son, Anthony Winston, about one mile from Tuscumbia, in Colbert county, in the direction of Sheffield. Anthony Winston, here mentioned on this tombstone, was the son of Anthony Winston of Hanover county, Virginia, who was born September 29th, 1723, and married February 29th, 1747, Alice Taylor, daughter of James Taylor and Alice Thornton. He was born in Hanover county, but moved in his young days to Buckingham county, Virginia. He was a captain in the Revolutionary War. He was married in 1776, and went into the army a few months afterwards.

The family has now in their possession a counterpane made of cotton which Mrs. Keziah Winston raised. She picked the cotton, spun the thread and wove the cloth, and then ornamented it by needle work like a Marseilles counterpane, whilst her husband was in the army. This old heirloom is perfectly preserved, and looks as well as it ever did, but of course, it is not used.

Anthony Winston told his grandchildren many things about the Revolutionary War, and particularly about General Washington. Some of these stories would not do to print, especially about the freedom with which "The Father of his Country" used the English language. But in his estimation no mortal man ever approximated General Washington as a great military chieftain. Sarah Winston, of Hanover, was the sister of Anthony Winston, of Hanover. She married John Henry and was the mother of Patrick Henry. Capt. Anthony Winston was sheriff of Buckingham county, Virginia, which office at that time was given to the oldest justice of the peace of the county for one term, under the law of Virginia. At that time a justice of the peace in Virginia received no pay, the principal business of that officer being to settle disputes among his neighbors without any lawsuit.

Alice Winston, the mother of Gen. Pettus, was born in Buckingham county, Virginia, but her father moved with his family about the beginning of the last century to Davidson county, Tennessee, and owned a plantation there, about one mile from the Hermitage. John Pettus was born in Fluvanna county, Virginia, near where Anthony Winston lived. He also moved to Davidson county, Tennessee, about the first of the last century. Alice Winston and John Pettus were married in Davidson county in 1807, and General Jackson danced at the wedding. And in the early days of Senator Pettus he was frequently at the "Hermitage" and heard General Jackson tell of the early life of his mother and father, and of his father's serving in the Creek War under him.